Love to Hate You, Hate to Love You

Gracelyn Ulula

BookLeaf Publishing

Presentation by *BookLeaf Publishing*

Web: www.bookleafpub.com

E-mail: info@bookleafpub.com

ISBN: 9789395026529

First edition 2022

Everything is always for my son Judah, but also for those who struggle with mental health issues.

Don't let anyone stop your healing, including yourself.

ACKNOWLEDGEMENT

Thank you to my family and my close friends old and new. You have gotten me through the worst time of my life and for you to still be there for me has saved me from myself. Thank you for everything, I hope you'll enjoy this book and find some poems that would comfort you.

PREFACE

Love to Hate You, Hate to Love You is a book of poetry written for a writer's challenge for BookLeaf Publishing to write a book in 21 days. This challenge comes perfectly on time as I begin to finally make a full recovery from an extreme psychosis/manic episode I had in December 2021. Each poem gives the reader a glimpse into the feelings and discoveries made through that experience. From it, I'm happy to have resolved many issues that I had not previously realized were controlling my life. It caused a lot of unnecessary anguish and muddled my true motivation in everything I did, thought and felt. These unprocessed emotions and traumas turned me into someone I no longer recognized. Though, I sought great change in 2020-2021 and achieved a lot in practice, all of that work only truly got set in stone by actually living life, loving and capturing each moment. The person I sought out to be was always who I truly was. What I failed to realize though, in absent and robotic acts of submission, was that this person that I so longed to be fully integrated with lay in who I constantly suppressed, not who I needed to magically turn into. What would have happened if you made a different choice? Who would you be if you did something different? If certain events never took place? Seeking change and healing turned ugly with personality splits, impulsiveness, irresponsibility, manipulation, dishonesty and a lot of self hatred for my life thus far. As you grow-up,you learn and change naturally, yes, but to change who you are at your core is to be someone you simply can never become. Thinking about it now, seems to be an extremely far-fetched notion and useless pursuit. Now, life has become much simpler, happier and filled with the love I so desperately sought after. No where close to the end, I'm always getting better, but only finding everything I ever needed by remaining present and remaining thankful for it. Getting here was only harder because of my own stubbornness and fear of facing myself. I hope that my words could help you on your own journey to self discovery and true happiness. Thank you for reading and sharing this journey and feelings with me.

Save Yourself

Welcome to America
Where rape culture ensues
Taking away everything you have
Leaving you with nothing
But violence from violation
From war cries of my ancestors
Of love only given
If something is offered
Never a two way street
No milk and honey
Only Terrorism and revenge
From a people that will never forgive
"I'll show them!"
Blame everyone,but yourself
Show em,you're better
By always being alone
Isolating and migrating
Staying nowhere
Finding endless circles
Of insanity for a little girl
That won't believe
That people will forever be evil
Constantly praying
For someone to be different
For anyone to listen
Anyone to believe
Only finding herself left again

Doing all manners of evil
Against herself
Self sabotaging and dismantling
Everything she holds good and true
Giving it up over and over again
Because someone told her
Love was sacrifice
Not justice
Because someone told her
Loving yourself was selfish
Everyone in the world
deserves to know this pain
Of perfection and domestication
That comes with knowing better
Of a relationship
Of the fairy tales we were promised
That you want so desperately
But could never grasp gracefully
Unwilling to tell the truth
Terrified you'll get
all that you deserve
Afraid of being wrong
More afraid of the wars you started
Actually being acted upon
This wrath ensues
It's boils up and up
to a point of choking out
your child you'll never have
So they will never do

All of these same mistakes again
Praying to God
No one falls in love with my baby
And takes everything
good you have
Because innocence is irresistible
True love and Goodness is rare
It's a power move
If you believe and receive
something they want
Without doing anything
Undeservingly stealing from heaven
Like you stole from me
But were given graciously
Praying one day you'd do
something about it
That you'd learn love
 in crippling you
In saving you from the pain of living
From the pain of the truth
Holding onto ignorant bliss
To get you to keep
the economy going
Because we must
keep each other alive
Eternally damned to serve
Alone forever being
The love you give yourself
Too afraid of any risk of heartbreak

Risk of investment
Risk of having something
 that can be lost
That'd ruin your future
That would tear your world apart
If I store my heart
somewhere that can't be found
Maybe I'll escape it all
infinity ending this nightmare
That is a utopia
Once and for all
"God save us"
Never finding the ability
To save yourself

Eden's Eve

Am I evil?
Did I cause this beautiful disaster?
Am I unforgivable?
Am I irreversible?
Am I wrong for having no borders?
No limits of love or creation?
Creating anything that crossed
My heart and mind
in innocent wonder
Will you show me the truth?
Will you lead me to the cross?
Are you going to
teach me how to love truly?
Are you going to make me pure?
Am I everything you hate?
Everything unholy?
All of the things
that no one would listen to
throughout history
Begging to avoid pain
Begging to stop
self serving selfishness
Life would be so much easier
If they never had

to deal with their existence
Think of the children
Who never asked for this
If only you would of been honest
If only you would of been less selfish
If only you knew what love is
To escape this utopian dictatorship
Begging God for answers
Wondering without identity
Flying without any direction
Straight into all of nothingness
If only you would of listened
If only you would of learned
What happened to you?
What went wrong?
Needing some actual truth
Needing some understanding
Needing someone who
knew something about reality
Narcissistic control issues
Anger and disgust of sin
Self punishing
violence of submission
Learning to love the pain
of force, obedience and sacrifice
Eating forbidden fruit mindlessly
for something sweet
Falling from Grace
from listening to

the Christian devil
Promising reward
for all this rape
Who never saw
anything of value
Of the life of God's creation
Of the body breathing together
believing it needs
to be purified
Not knowing anything
of purity and love but only
cult sacrificial violence
But the original love of Adam
Following Eve to her damn-nation
The only one not appalled
at her dismissal
Listening to her
misguided innocence
because he loved her
Like Jesus sacrificed himself
Adam walked into hell with his lover
Going after the 1
Leaving the 99
Shepherd my fallen ones
Seeking and finding true love
To be restored
That they tried to destroy
Promising they weren't good enough
All the little children

Back into their eden
Save our children
Save our innocence
From sodom and Gomorrah

Living Universe Love

The rise is always
greater than the fall
I die everyday
and come back to life
by your embrace
Leaving everything behind
Including you daily
Praying to God
That you'll come back to me
Praying to God
That you're truly mine to stay
Trusting your great escape
Was more of a short vacation
Maybe next time
we can find our
momentary paradise
together for a day
Find it when I'm with you
In bouts of Union
In ripping up weeds
In gardening my mind
In planting of seeds
In reaping a great harvest
That will last us
through the tougher times
When I can't sleep

When I'm losing everything
Trusting you to find me
in my space
Bring the sun into the galaxy
Remind me life is not
just blood and sacrifice
But life and justice
In the form of forgiveness
In the form of creation
In the form of loving thyself
In loving you
In letting you go
In letting everything
that takes a hold
Be as it may
Elevate to new worlds
Coming into new realities
Changing timelines
with our intimacy
Leaving and choosing you
Having everything and nothing
Offered the world
And choosing love
Honey, I can be
your everything
I can be your nothing
I can be your great escape
Your savior or
your greatest enemy

I can be your bitch
I can be your queen
We can be Gods of the universe
And the devils of this hell on earth
I will be your fortress
Your home and your world
Your hell on earth
 as it is in heaven
I can be your sex slave
Your servant
The most annoying person
you've ever met
The biggest liar of them all
The most grotesque
Obama-nation
That just wants you to live
I will give you freedom
I will give you peace
I will give you everything
And if I give you nothing
Would you still choose me?
if I gave you everything
Without giving you anything
If I gave you love
Would that be enough?
If I gave you myself
Would you be able to love me?
Like I'm trying to love myself,
Like I'm trying to love you?

Choosing Nothing

Would you be able
to choose me?
Do you even want me?
Can you even stand me?
Being everything
 that you hate
Everything wrong and right
and nothing at all
Full of violence
and peace and harmony
Full of chaos and destruction
Full of sweet rebellion and lust
Calling your Demons awake
asking you to do something
Asking you to stop
following suit
Earth, shaking and quaking
And sweet lust and sex
And sweet power and dominance
In a game of Ying and yang
finding everything and nothing
In perfect independence,
needing each other
and needing nothing at all
Giving power to self
but giving power to each other

Knowing that you need
one another
While not needing
 anything at all
Perfectly content alone
Yet choosing what you need
 and everything that you wanted
getting the best of both worlds
But is it the world that you
truly belong in?
Your home that
you never found
The Eden that you
were cast out of
Only finding
perfection and snakes
that tell you that you're
not good enough
That ask you for improvement
Leaving out all
mistakes and humanity
As not being worthy
as not being able to handle it
Not knowing where
to even begin
an attempt at capturing it
And instead choosing
to just let go
and find peace within self

and whatever may flow
I'm yours if you choose me
and I'm yours if you don't
Asking to be released
trusting to always return
Building a little faith
out of this broken cult
Can we be trusted
with the universe?
It will be released
like I release you to be free
do and be as you please
See you in the next reality

Pure expectation

No one saw me
as valuable as anything
spectacular, besides
my perfect performance
Guaranteed silence
not wondering what kind
of things are happening
in my brain, spirit, heart
mind, soul, & body
just too concerned
with making sure
that I don't appearimpure
and I seem to bethe perfect
embodiment of Christ
and that there is no
Actual relationship
nothing actually intimate
making sure that they
can take and take and take
until there's nothing left
for me in the end
always wondering when
I get to speak
if I'm able to at all
not worried about
who I am or what I need

Leaving nolove for myself
and disregarding sacrifice
Being nothing because
that's what they want me to do
as long as I produce
giving them money to live their life
and save them
from their own damnnation
when I was the one
that needed saving
and that was their responsibility
when I was a child
and I needed the things
that I needed and
they withheld it from me
 I didn't learn anything
And ended up becoming nobody
completely stripped of identity
with nothing to lean on
except the good word
without direction or understanding
only perfect belief, faith and worship
and nothing else to go on
no direction of right and wrong
upside, down, backwards or in between
and side to side confusion
going in all directions
of time and space and wander
creating happiness and anger

too afraid to make a mistake
to ever tell the truth or be known
afraid of my own shadow
and it being the only thing
that gives me comfort
following whispers
inviting in things I didn't understand
why am I being tortured?
who let these demons in?
Why was I the host of everything
To be trusted with everything
Only destroying everything I love
From not knowing how to keep it safe
Finding no love here
only the burning of hell
But like a Phoenix
rising from the ashes
From lies of deception
that the devil so carefully constructed
to keep us from freedom and love
True intimacy and relationship
From everything good
that was our garden
of peace and rest as if
that wasn't good enough
Be careful what you wish for
Because you may not be able
to live with yourself
From the decisions you've made

Creating a life you hated
Never dreamed of living
Finding nothing you like or love
Holding onto safety, Mediocracy
lies of contentment
Getting all you ever wanted
Without love, sacrifice or work
Never living simply
Never knowing who
you were created to be
Only self serving mundane
Automatic, cold professional economy

Loving you letting go

I don't want to capture you
I refuse to possess you
Please don't let me
take up any space
Discard of me after I leave
Don't let me affect anything
I couldn't bare
the burden of ruining you
The thought of disrupting
your life makes
my stomach upset
Even thinking of you
 for a moment
I couldn't possibly use you
For escape and a way
to live again
I'm never going to
get lost this way
Please don't give
your heart to me
Rip out any idea
you had of before
Start the day over
and get to know me now
Don't allow this connection
to stop flowing

through every stream
Carefully calculating
without doing anything
But just existing
In close proximity
Please don't hide
away from me
Driving wedges
between everything
I can't be #goals with you
Don't sum me up
to checked boxes and rules
On your perfect
well planned future
Picking until there's
nothing left
 to be discovered
Give me space to breath
Leave me alone
with myself to heal
Come on strong
Then leave me
with a good cliff hanger
Don't be shaken by me
Paranoid self made fears
Cannot make a home there
Clean yourself of me
Please don't dream of
forever right now

And miss all
of this holiness
Believe me now
That the person I was
Has ceased to exist
Live with me now
Don't breath life
into who I was
when we first met
Please don't get
stuck on me
Hung up on
all the pretty ideas
Of what love is
And fantasies
you made up
Surely I must be dreaming
Unbelievably undeserving
Unworthy of everything
you ever wanted
I beg of you
don't get lost in fears
Holding onto safety
for the life of you
Going about unchanged
unaffected disconnected
safely already dead
to pain and all feeling
I can't bare the thought

Of ever destroying you
Ever changing your
already perfect humanity
Can't breath
if I took it from you
If I did anything to
take you away
from who you are
I can't be the reason for pain
Don't allow me to be
Why you did
anything differently
Please don't settle
for anything
Take zero shit
don't allow me in
I will surely disappoint
you in the end
If you thought
for an instant
That this was it
Don't let me
persuade you
I cannot be
what convinced You
of anything
Different from who
you are made to be
Don't let me become

Any part of you
No high horses,
or pedi-stools
Please I can't be
The world to you
They said if you love a flower
Don't pick it
Let it live and grow
exactly where you found it
And I will let you be
And simply admire
Everything that makes up
The person in front of me
 Can you trust me
To let you live
As you are constantly?
Will it be okay
If connecting
Took time and
all of eternity?
Could you love me truly?
Enough to let me go
Without fear?
Believe nothing can change
What we have between us
That no matter what
What we have
Nothing could possibly
Threaten to disrupt it

A connection like this
Comes once or twice
In a life time
Would you be
brave enough
to actually have it?
and not subconsciously
Destroy it?
From pain undiscovered
And questions unanswered
Unspoken wonderings
And firewalls for your safety
No risk, no reward
I will never hurt you
Because I can no longer
hurt myself
No more begging
for punishment
No seeking violence
No more fantasies of pain
I will possess your heart

Living Energy

The wind is my friend
In this sunshine
The trees raising
their hands in praise
They are my congregation
The flower turning
Towards rays of light
Is where I find understanding
Graduate from buildings
And forced relationships
From performance
And proving points
Choosing the right thing
By being yourself
And expecting nothing less
Than mutual respect
Sit with me a little longer
Come alive as we breath
in all of the things
We've been trying
to get away from
Exasperation and desperation
End much sooner
Than we expect
Afraid our fears are true
Delighted to know
They can't hurt us

When we're with you
Embracing the feeling we get
As we gaze upon the way
The light is reflected
From your complexion
Loving all of creation
Without guilt or shame
Of not being worthy yet
Giving yourself the universe
That you could never accept
But slowly taking in
As you are able and willing
Through pain you didn't see
Processing that which was
never given energy
Confusion that left you all alone
Finding peace and love
As the storm is over
Flowers bloom
The filter over your eyes
Seemingly shift
 from black and white
To vibrant full blown color
No longer willing
To give energy to the unworthy
Or life to those things
That seek some violent ending
To all of this beautiful living
That they will never be worthy of

Forgive me son

Forgive me son
For the mistakes I've made
For wanting you so badly
That I hurt myself to get you
You were all I ever wanted
And I wanted you so selfishly
I was so greedy and I got lost
I needed you to save me
Forgive me for needing you like that
For using you
For something I couldn't do
That broke me timelessly
Over and over again
I was too afraid to build a family
Because it meant that I could lose it
I wanted it prematurely
Unable to find any relief
Besides going after you endlessly
Forgive me son
I promise you
that you were worth it
Don't believe the quiver
in my voice
Please trust the tears
Were well deserved
Know that everything

I gave for you
Was everything I needed to live
I needed to go through
To finally find myself again
And be here with you
Don't blame me too much
Hatred is a given
If you knew the full truth
But don't pin good vs evil
Please don't do that to yourself
Know that I'm never mad at you
All of it is being
disappointed in myself
For doing this to you
Trust me when I say
You were worth every sacrifice
And heart break
When you find out
about my dreams and aspirations
to be somewhere
outside of this universe
Please don't even think
you weren't a part of that
When you watch me
leave in the night
For a moment
Where I don't need to hide
To protect you constantly
Don't think I wouldn't rather

   hold you while you sleep
But loving you means
allowing us both a life outside of here
You have to be independent
When the weight
ofit is killing me
And you wonder
why I'm gone around
the same time of year
For a few days or weeks
Enjoy your extended family for me
Don't waste time missing me
Or wondering if I'll be alright
Know that in this short vacation
We are both healing
In whatever we're individually doing
When you finally ask for the truth
That you instinctively
Have known since the day I met you
I pray is that is the day
you'll be able to carry
 this load with me
But I hope you know
That it's not your responsibility
I just pray you wouldn't hate yourself
Or blame yourself for any of it
I needed you, yes
But honey I wanted you
more than anything

God knew I needed you too
So he sent you to save me from myself
So you see?
Forgive me son
Forgive me for needing a savior at all
For my inability
to save myself at the time
I just needed some motivation
I needed to give you all of my love
It needed somewhere to go
So I created you desperately
Prematurely, poorly, alone
My emotional tether was fractured
I was losing consciousness
For that I am so gravely sorry
I hope one day
you'll read this and know
You are not a villain
that destroyed your hero
No no no
Forgive me son
For making you
the hero in this story
Forgive me for actually
being the damsel in distress
the princess in a castle
The wallflower no one came after
Forgive me for
dreaming of you too soon

For not being ready yet
For running from you
For needing to heal
For not being myself
but needing to find it
after you were already here
I've begged God for forgiveness
But now?
I'm asking you
Forgive me son
For it having to be like this
But know I would do it again
Just to get back to you
Because you are worth all of it
And I truly love you
I hope I haven't failed you
Know that I'm here
I'll never leave again
Even if it seems that way
In the seasons of separation
 Believe me when I admit
You were the dream I wanted
I don't want to be
anywhere else more
than this life by your side
 In our perfect and
 imperfect little family
 Forgive me son
 For that being a story

That will greatly affect our lives
Through all of time
You can get out of this loop
By knowing the truth
I was just trying to
build a legacy for you
But failed to realize
The cost of anything
Forgive me son
For needing to be
both nurturer and provider
For needing to go away sometimes
I find myself when I disconnect
I wish you really could
Give me everything I need
In order to truly feel alive
But I was given something better
Someone to live for
A reason to remain in a place
That's good for you
I refuse to be taken away
No more great escapes
No desperate stunts
To be noticed and given attention
No more begging
the people around me
To listen to all of my heart ache
I receive from living
I have everything I need

Right here, right now
Especially when we finally
Get to be together
After long days of separation
And going away on vacation
No more ventures
And grandeur pursuits
Of happiness
That couldn't be further
from everything I've ever wanted
Forgive me son
For loving you
The only way that I knew
Immaturely, desperately, and fully
Please let it go
for the sake of yourself
In due time I will fully
 be known by you
Don't try to connect with me
Before you are ready
Don't look at others with envy
At mother's who maybe
could of been better for you
I dreamed of them too
I wondered if I was good enough
If we could stay together
So, forgive me son
For not being brave enough
To save you

From this impending heart break
From this ultimate
act of self sabotage
For being unable
to dream and the refusal
to keep wondering
Forgive me for not giving
you any form of paradise
for not being the perfect person
 I knew I could be for you
Instead, I decided that I would give you
Me and myself authentically
Unfortunately, the it's not very pretty
But the beauty I've lived and seen
That's all I intend to give to you
When you discover this tragedy
And wonder how
it didn't end in catastrophe
as any good story
of the genre should go
I hope that the part
that would also save you
Would hold you down
More than I could ever do
Forgive me son
For never giving away my dying heart again
For never knowing me fully
For only feeling my affection
For falling asleep in your arms

For running away
For needing breaks
For the secrets in the dark
For skeletons not kept very well
 in closets of discontentment
Forgive me for
 telling you the truth
I at least tried to tell you gracefully
I know it'll never be easy
But hold onto to every memory
you have of me
loving you completely
Use it to finally
Let go of what you thought of me
And please, forgive me son

Expectation Release

I've grown very comfortable
With everyone's general disinterest
I feel relieved actually
I don't like attention
or many people in general
So much hate and projection
It kills me in the end
What I am relieved about the most
Is probably what follows after
"How are you"
"Can I have more?"
"Can you do this for me?"
"Can I ask a favor",
"I need you",
"I'm relying on you"
"Can you help me?"
Busy working for community
Working for relationships and love
So busy that I failed to notice
No one was working for me
I was a slave
To everyone else's life
I didn't have one of my own
I became some remedy
A transaction that
 substituted closeness

No one actually
wanted to know
My dreams at night
There was no one
to laugh with me
at the jokes I told myself
When I needed help
or a remedy myself
I was left all alone on my own
The only person
I could count on
The only person
I could ever count on
Was the only one ever truly had
I wanted to be loved
and thought of so badly
The sum of my worth
based off of what I could do
for everyone else
So I tried to prove it
I'm worth knowing
I'm worth loving
I'm worth being here too
But the only person
I was trying to convince
was myself
Sure the help tried
to do what they could
They always get hurt in the end

But the help isn't very helpful
When you're unable
to help yourself
Give a dose of tough love
Call it the ending of a season
A natural transition
Of life lived and love lost
Letting everything
and everyone go
Forgetting about "the good times"
Dreaming of a happier time
Only remembering
what you need
to survive right now
You were praying
for the end back then
Now that you've come
to the other side
Of growing up
And healing from past
childish thinking
And done avoiding
all the emotional processing
that you would never
get over or tell the truth about
You're finally just being
Accepting all that means
Done working for the wind
Chasing things that can't exist

Accepted the truth
for whatever it is
Decided that your heart
will not break from this
And that protecting your energy
Isn't heartless or so cold after all
You're just keeping it safe
By keeping it for yourself
Only giving it to those
who dare to question
and actually want
the true answer
Satisfied with your loneliness
Finding true friends
Without bad intention
Recognizing the ones
with good motivation
Not being so shaken
by the amount of people
who wish me ill anymore
Unconcerned with their desires
To unlock all of the life inside of me
Disgusted by their desire at all
"You make me feel alive"
"I like talking to you"
"I could stare at your face all day"
"I just imagine all the things
I want to do to you."
As if that's all I'm good for

Like it's my job to give you
satisfaction in your existence
Give you that tingly feeling
You don't feel anywhere else
Completely uninterested
in who I actually am
No genuine conversation
or connection
Just there.
 Just wanted to see your smile
Just wanted your embrace really quick
Can't say no or have any opinion
No questions of how I feel
Or what I think of you as well
Tire me out until I have none left
Only working for my compliance
Never allowing me to exist

Haunting Me

I saw you today
I swear it was you
Haunting everything I do
Trying to forget and move on
Take a minute and breathe
Talk yourself off the cliff
Quiet the racing thoughts
Forget the hate you received
Disconnect from the weight of it
Don't get lost in how
this person affected everything
Avoid tangents of blame
And regret
Reclaim the power you gave over
To be so infected by them
Take responsibility for your actions
Accept your decision in this
Being led to roads you
could never have known
That distorted everything
Destroyed all innocence
And everything good
Accept you got what you deserved
You saw and heard
The way he moves
Choosing to still love him in the end

Even if that meant
The sacrifice of you
Incapable of loving you back
Not knowing the half of it
How to do it correctly
Too afraid of ruining everything
You're greatest mess
The person who loved you most
And didn't know how
to let it out correctly
Taking it out on yourself
At the refusal to get
anymore involved
The back and forth
Constant confusion
Ruining my head
Leaving only distress
Distrust of anything
I know and feel
Creating the person
You wanted so badly
But didn't have the balls
To love correctly
Running into the arms of safety
Do not come back here
Don't let anyone here

Poetry

Often I'll speak
in rhyme and confusion.
In contradictions,
tricks of amusement.
Walking mess,
standing ovations
of the human condition
looking for some kind of solution.
An Obama-nation
looking for some civilization.
Simply complicated
and eternally something undefined.
Go down the rabbit hole
if you must.
Wake up to something
you find isn't so different
from imagination
and games we love so much

Death of Savior Complex

If you're searching
for a savior
I promise you
that I'm not it
No credit or glory
for your greatness
You don't have to worry
I'm not going
to hold it over you
I can't be why
you made anything
No muse or inspiration
Saving lives and
changing timelines
Become too serious
People get obsessive
Pervert you
and expect relationship
Expectation forced behavior
Consistency to keep the legacy
Knowing the rules you keep
Playing each string
Watching me dance delightfully
Using me for everything
Bringing momentary relief
From all your self loathing

Curbing the inevitable
Giving you a little more time
Or encouraging
your self destruction
You decide how you want to react
Take it too personally
Unable to imagine
the bigger picture
Despising the role you're given
Feeding jealousy
and all matters of evil
Unable to see how to
use it for the greater good
Forever believing
 everyone else
That you were made useless
Succumbing to their abuse
Shutting your ears
repeating what they told you
"They gave me an identity
I could understand
Something I could read about
in scientific studies"
Capping your ability
Telling yourself lies
Of being completely worthless
Subscribing to co-dependance
Refusing to change or adapt
Waiting and accepting help

"Maybe today I'll find happiness
Today I'll find relief
From my existence"
Giving yourself
the same punishment
Expecting to feel different
Maybe if I do something else
Trying to work your way
into paradise, forgiveness,
peace and rest
Actively avoiding home
Letting every micro inconvenience
Obliterate all your progress
"God why are you
testing me like this?"
No self management
Giving all your energy into everything
Avoiding yourself most of all
Not leaving
an ounce for yourself
Forever working for something
No one else
on earth can give you
Until you receive it
And stop self sabotaging
Stop the conversation
That feeds fear, lies,
 violence and chaos
No entertaining foreign thinking

Start questioning everything
Why am I like this?
What put me on this path
Keep the course
Leave all distraction
No more faking it to make it
You either do or you don't
Finally accept it
Finding absolution in love
And the way
you give it to yourself
Finally taking your power back
And claiming it proudly
You don't get to tell me
who I am any more
I know now
Break out of all the boxes
They force you into
Too afraid of discovery
Lacking adventure and curiosity
No sense of wonder or adventure
All bravery completely
out the window
You are the universe
Stop giving cowards
 any glimpse of it
Contentment and middle ground
Is here, right now
Living in the present

Sensing senses

I didn't come for the money
I didn't come as a survival tactic
I made you this because I loved you
I just wanted to see your face
I wanted to see your reaction
To my spice combination
What do you think of this wine pairing?
I'm exploring my senses lately in creating
I wanted to hear how you felt lately
I was wondering if you were happy
Is where your living supporting you?
Are they being nice to you?
I was just wondering
Did you process that correctly?
Did you deal with this yet?
Is it steering you to places
That are good for you?
Were you really listening?
Or did you hear what you wanted to?
I know I talk too much
I ask too many questions
I was just wondering
Are you still heartbroken
by the person that lied to you?
That told you all those sweet nothings
That gave you hopes and dreams

You thought you could live on
When you needed meat
When protein takes so much work
And they were severely unwilling
But they also didn't know
What you meant exactly
They didn't want to
I was just wondering
Oh, maybe you would rather sleep
It's much easier to escape
Not worth saving
So, rest your dying head
Go down quickly
Knowing about everything
Or claiming to
When you're trying to know nothing
The dying light wasn't worth
enough to you
Ignorance is bliss
Don't be a hero
Let someone else live
Their savior complex
You hand it off to other people
Let someone else carry
the world for once
Making sense
Or blabbering like an idiot
Who are you to judge?
You finally catch up on sleep

Just to lose it for the next week
can't win for losing
Why isn't it ever enough
Honey it will never be
So rest easy
Stop giving so many fucks
They don't come around anymore
The cold sweats got them tired
Dinner will be ready in a moment dear
But it was never enjoyed
Never savored
They couldn't even
begin to taste the flavor
but everyone's gotta eat

Utopian earth

Search for eyes
Looking into windows
Shopping for satisfaction
Finding lies of sweet hospitality
Transactions of love
Business as usual
Peace and utopian rule
Throw away the pain
Silence the humanity
Shame the purity
Guilt my enjoyment and pleasure
Everything good is bad
Everything wrong is right
Which one is it?
Serve your master dog
Keep working for a treat
Mammal, serpent, simple
Get this if you give that
Losing everything
Gaining nothing
Rape culture swarms
Cancel culture disconnects
What are the solutions?
Savior complex reunions
Lives lost in a rat race
Crippling infants to take

credit for their success
"Killing me softly with your lies"
Can't look into your eyes
As I watch them
Killing you softly
And you taking it willingly
For moments of satisfaction
Glimpses of living
Putting away all of yourself
To make everyone else happy
Putting on a good face
Call it surviving
Pretend to fit in
Curve the void
Swallow the empty conversation
With your medication
Praying they don't drug you again
Trying to hold onto
Slivers of say so
Of freedom
Coming back down silently
In secret, taking deep breaths
 and healing
Without being too revealing

Crimes against you

Look at what they did to you
They told you the rules
Of what you can and can't do
Brainwashed and abused
Used to be their dog
For whatever evil they can use
Forced into submission
Into their everyday judgement
Wrong vs right
Good vs evil
Not giving people
the choice for themselves
Who are we to judge?
Who are we to take action
without seeing the bigger picture
Not knowing who this person is
Thinking they are not worthy
That they're incapable of change
Taking away their future
As if that's our job to save
Or escape or move with the spirit
That gives us permission
That asks us if we would still serve him
If we give up everything
If we do all manners of evil
Would we remain

a good and diligent servant
Not questioning our motivation
Not following the good word
Listening to our emotions
Without praise and worship
Without reading
the wisdom and truth
Of our creator
Serving our own impulses
Following money and
not that which is holy
Getting sold lies of control
Lies of rewards equalling
Your land of milk and honey
In this paradise we call
land of the free
As long as you submit
To every rule, law and commandment
Forcing perfection and beauty
Queen don't fall for it
King don't stand on it
This utopia can't last forever
Cries of violation are built on it
Begging for true justice
Begging for forgiveness
in place of sacrifice
In place of survivorship
Catching the most innocent of us
Giving us an escape

Run run away
And never come back
To this hell they promised us
Was the dream worth living
As if ours wasn't good enough
Cursed by your ancestors
Cursed by all this hatred and violence
Knowing exactly what you need
And never being able to capture it
You being evil
Never being able to admit it
Never wanting to repent and change
Only wanting what's best for you
Only wanting selfish gain
Never going against the grain
Never loving in a way that is above men
Giving everything you have up
To live forever
Never giving God anything
Ending up with nothing
Ending it all by falling
on your own sword
As if sacrifice was still
the game we're playing
Like Jesus didn't do that already
Like justice wasn't
the new rules of your lane
Mistaking the water and blood
For literally taking every name

The war is over
The spirits are our domain
Listen, feel, pray, meditate
The burden is no longer yours to bear
Create whatever you need
I just hope that that's also what you want
So that it's something real
Not some sad escape from yourself
Escape from reality
Escape from this evil
Escape from knowledge
From God,
from family
from everything
that's worth something
Don't hurt yourself
Escaping to plastic beaches
With your plastic body
Certainly I've made it
To the next level of serenity
Finding nothing but
your consciousness
Telling you the truth
Telling you what you need
Telling you what you want
Asking you to be good
And you being incapable of it
Forgive me father for I have sinned
Forgive them father for

they know not what they do
Teach us to be new
Teach us to finally be
satisfied with the truth
Satisfied with who we actually are
She devil… white devil…
Angel of death
Mother Nature
Adam and Eve running
banished from the garden of Eden
Forever searching for each other
And never finding
Ending up in abuse and toxic
Identity issues
Surely this is the love
I've been waiting for
Discarded the moment you mess up
Not good enough
I'll find someone who is
I never really loved you
I only loved myself
You don't know what love is honey
You just do what your told
You just go along to get along
You're not brave, or strong,
or special or anything good at all
You are evil, without love or truth
God is love, God is good
Without God you are nothing

Can you live with yourself?
Can you truly love yourself
In all your sin and humanity
Knowing you deserve death
You deserve to go to hell
And still love so much
That you would never
cross God ever again
Because you couldn't
live with yourself
Would you still serve me?
If you were given
all of your hearts desires
Everything you manifested
As the God of your own universe
The shaper of all things "good"
You devil and evil no gooder
Giving yourself lies of submission
Not knowing what you truly need
What you truly want
Outside of their abuse
You don't know what love is
You can't handle the truth
Love so good that's
keeping you alive
That's waiting to be realized
Realizing it
Still serving your own sin
God patiently waiting

For his children to finally
love him back
Waiting for all of eternity
For something that
can never happen
Forgive us father for
we know not what we do
We are nothing without you
We are nothing at all
I do not exist
Neither do you
Who is holy among you?
Who is worthy?
Self hatred eating you alive
Be refreshed
Be renewed
Kill your flesh in the spirit
Be who you are in God
And God alone

Burdens of Healing

Someone stop my bleeding heart
I don't want to feel this weak
Connecting is what I'm afraid of
Seeing what you see
is what I'm avoiding
Holding onto pain
that lives inside of you
Living it over and over again
Disrupting your stream
of consciousness
Ruining vacations
with uncomfortable conversations
Cries of slavery and injustice unseen
Praying for rain
When it's sunny
And you have no more sweat
No more toxins to leave your body
Building walls so high
For all of them to come crashing down
Having to start over constantly
Trying to stop the bleeding
Praying that no one sees
Trying not to think too loudly
Just wanting to coast by unnoticed
Swearing that you're done listening
Just trying to live with yourself

So you take a break and disconnect
Sure we had some good laughs
Your stupidity tickled me
My ignorance felt like serenity
Space filled itself this time
Another void created
Needing something more
Craving something sustainable
Feeling the loneliness again
Knocking at my door
Is that you God?
Angel of death?
Something more scary?
Constantly giving yourself
Mini heart attacks
Was this normal?
Did I just have a Seizure?
Something broke inside of me
Can you hear the pop?
Did you see the lights last night?
What did they tell you to do this time?
Listening to different frequencies
Leaning on your own waves
Tired of surfing
Whatever helps you
sleep at night right?
Hit another blunt
Run another mile
Pray for a real friend

Hold onto every penny they take
Then give it all away
Heart broken, cold, stagnant
Going nowhere
Finding happiness everywhere
Along with your heart
You thought you lost
Bleeding too much
Over someone who didn't give af
Can't beat 'em join 'em
Just trying not to get lost
But you do
So you try something else
Make me stop
God will it ever stop
I'm just trying to live with myself
Both constantly caring
And not giving a fuck
My balance is
a never ending backwards
Up and down
Space gone both felt
 and numbed out
Figuring it out
Art is free
So I give you my mind and heart
Because it will never leave
It will always stay with me
Again, I will come back

Love to hate me
Hate to love me
Just hoping you wouldn't run away
Don't let that hatred sabotage you
Don't let me reflect you
Do you like yourself?
Because I sure liked you
I hated the self hatred
The vain self glory
The pain you put yourself through
The way you did you
Hated myself too
Spilling everything I needed
Should of been more careful
Too stupid to learn anything new
Trying to feel again
This ice is not comfortable
Just trying to warm up a little
Feel something
Do nothing
Trying to escape
Loops of time and history
Trying to remember
Navigating through the bullshit
Just trying to hold onto belief
Hold onto self
Hold onto positivity
Hold onto to living
What do you do

when you feel everything?
How does it feel
to harness the power of the universe?
Control freak
Psychosis moments
I promise you
you aren't a worthy sacrifice
You're too precious
to be stopped in your tracks
Did you finally find yourself?
Did you recognize it at all?
Those things aren't you
Can't you see
what they're doing to you?
I can't look anymore
I only see you
Bringing the storm
Controlling the rain
So much energy
Can you harness it correctly?
No one should be allowed that power
Who can be trusted with it?
Who is worthy among you?
I don't want it
I can't even trust myself
Someone stop me
Getting your wildest death wish
Death not even interested
Not even the devil

offers comfort anymore
Running into the arms of an Angel
Running away from the original
Finding escapes
Punching in cheat codes
Call me a hacker
Call me a fake, A fraud, a liar
Best of all call me a sinner
When you only lie to yourself
Can't even tell the reality
through your fortune telling phases
Of insecurity and hatred
For the inability and refusal
You go through
Do to yourself
Why can't you love you?
You need me I don't need you
Call me a hieratic
Call me the devil herself
Call me goddess
Mother Nature
Tafeti harnessing all creation in one body
Spitefully used and abuse
Turned into a monster
From someone who couldn't love her
Failing to know what it even is
Praise that which
you can't stop thinking about
Gravity moving you closer to me

I need you so much closer
The only eyes that drives me wild
Praying it's yours
Scared what it'll mean if it's not
What did you do?
How could you do this to her?
Praying to God
They don't come after you
Everything you ever wished for
Praying for violence
Praying for an ending to the sirens
Your wish is my command
Be careful what you wish for
Don't use God that way
Couldn't you let go for a moment?
Why didn't you believe?
Do you really have so much trust issues
That you ruined everything
You had the world you wanted
Finally made it to your destination
Why didn't you want it?
Silly human
Tricks are for kids
Time to grow up now
You cannot escape
You're doing everything so right
You will never escape
So keep living
Escape the zombies

wake the robots
Befriend the monsters
Ask them

Enough yet

Am I good enough yet?
Would you still want me if I'm upset?
If I step on your toes and
get you riled up?
If I can't stop weeping
from the climate?
Would you hold my hand
when I'm afraid at night
Would you embrace me
when I want to fight?
Would you love me
when my hair is a wreck
If I could barely get dressed?
Would I be good enough then?
If I did everything perfectly
Crossed the t's and dotted my I's
Put on a perfect performance
Gave you everything you wanted
If I looked you in the eye
Smirked approximately on Q
Giggled quietly at your jokes
Maintained my perfect figure
Became the girl you always dreamed
Would you still love me if I wasn't?
If I got it wrong
If I wasn't good at all

If I yelled at you and
threw the biggest tantrum
Got too drunk and acted like a fool?
If I broke under the pressure
you put me through
Lost my mind and still came back to you?
Would you love me
if I went away for a while?
Lost in mind mazes
that I call a personality
Give you enough energy to power a city
Would that scare you away from me?
Would you be able to
trust me in my chaos
In my frustrated nothingness?
Can you trust me
not to inflict harm intentionally
Do I even know what that is exactly?
Can you love me and see
that I need to get through this
Would you still be there for me
on the other side of it?
Would you ask me to change
and be something unrecognizable?
Be something prettier
More understood by the general public
Something more polite
Less confrontational
Would you still love me

if I made a mistake?
If I gave into temptation
If I did what I wanted to
And told you to fuck off
Let me live a little
If I stopped being afraid
of your judgement
Would you accept me as I am
If I got lost in my emotions
Listened to the wrong thing
Heard something incorrectly
Lost touch with my body
Escaped time and space
Went off in another dimension
And got taken over momentarily
Would you trust
 that I would return safely?
That it happened, it happens
That it's part of history
And part of avoiding the repetition of it
Is remembering it very vibrantly
To let it go
And be able to learn something new
To learn to do better
Would you trust that even in the chaos
In the drought, deserts, famine and war
That spring is coming?
That waters will flow again
That peace can exist

That harmony is learning
Growing In Humanity
Elevating through
all the world's distress
Coming back stronger than ever
Reborn into something better
A safer reality switch
Can you hold onto to me
While letting me go constantly?
Do you have enough love in your heart
To get your hands dirty with me?
To live and survive
And whatever that means through time?
Walk to the edge of existence with me
Hold your breath
And then breath more easy
Breath in the ocean
Move with the waves
Come alive with me under the moonlight
Would you still love me as I am?
Through all of my ugly humanity?

Worth something romantic

When will it be enough?
Dress more sexy
Do your hair in a different way
Maybe If your hips were wider
Skin darker, or skin lighter
Find that perfect golden brown
A good in between
maybe both?

If you got your nails done
Smiled more often
If only you didn't complain so much
You should of cooked everyday
Cleaned until your hands were raw
Maybe if you wore those sexy underwear
Waxed away every hair
Well, if that dark spot wasn't there
If you laughed more ladylike
Didn't speak up so much
Talked more respectfully
If only your tone wasn't so chilling
Tongue cutting like a sword
Maybe if you wore
high heels everywhere
So we can all admire
the arch in your back

If only your clothes were tighter
Show us your full form

I like my lashes fake
Even better with silicon titties
Don't worry about the side effects
Give me fake contacts
Perfection in artificial enhancement
Oh, your jaw could be pointier
If only your bone structure were sharper
Maybe if you did everything right
Happy all the time
Didn't have a problem with anything
Maybe then you'll finally
be worthy of love

Perhaps then you'll be
good enough for togetherness
If you only showered everyday
Dressed a certain way
Were more something else completely
If only you weren't you
Maybe then I'll finally
give you what you need
Let you live in peace
Then you can sleep at ease
Being whomever you please
If you did everything right
Put on the perfect performance

To earn all of my kindness
Respect, honor, glory, forgiveness
Love, communication, admiration
Loyalty and friendship

Would that be something you wanted?
Would there finally be
some reciprocation
Some two way street?
Some kind of Union
Could I come home restored
Would you finally say
that you're proud of me
That you see me fully
Would I then be valued
Cherished by you?
Is that when you can stand me?
When you won't go running away?
If I was your fantasy girl
Is that when you'd finally
stop looking elsewhere?
Is who I am right here
good enough

Would you stop wondering
where I'm heading?
Finally finding happiness
In your present, in reality
realizing that fantasies

were for escaping
No one likes to stay on vacation
I need you to run to me
Not away from everything
We can joke and play
But what do I really want?
Escape the rat race
Run away from all
forms of control that keeps
our minds in captivity
Stop everything
that seeks destruction
And finally just be

When the world tells you
to be something your not
And you get tired of running
away from home
Will you just be with me?
In all our imperfection
Would you come home?
And actually want to stay?
No avoiding, coping, no vacations, escaping,
disconnection, reflection
No disassociating, auto pilot, distractions
Just you and me being together
Would that be good enough finally?
If the only thing
you got out of it was me?

would I be
worth loving

Wonder

Do you wonder about me?
Do you go searching
for me in your sleep?
Are you alive
in moments we share?
Do you get stuck there?
Catch and release
Energy brewing and steaming
Finding no way through
Extinguished in
searching for meaning
Coming out in ways
that don't need to be explained
Too afraid to connect again
Fearing the triggers
Not allowed to become the world
Too powerful to be handled
Maybe enjoyed and admired
But to become something more?
I don't even know how to do it
Feelings over taken
Shaking the earth with energy
Changing the weather patterns
Praying to remain in control
Telling them you won't
get swept away again

You won't let it consume everything
A sacrifice this great
Is only reserved for one being
No more giving everything
Projections can't live in the present
Can't force gravity
Or time to move more quickly
Unknowingly going through the motions
Just trying to enjoy it while it's here
Don't break your own heart
From the inability to capture it
Refusal to accept things
you need the most
Can't recognize what
you want and need
even if it was there all along
Afraid of asking too many questions
Picking until you ruin it
Is this what I dreamed?
Have I finally made it?
Am I finally redeemed?
Can I return back to my inheritance?
Family matters turn to disaster
Tribes and villages
find no more connection
Lost in the hive of the collective
Why can't I tell you the truth
Hiding away until
you prove something more

Waiting to see if you feel the same
Will you take something out on me?
Lost in your own reflection
Can you successfully
Jump through to a new timeline?
Am I finally saved
Will I have something more
Finally trusted with someone
The tests of love and relationship
Navigating and losing every time
Cast out or protected?
Kept safe and dormant
In order to avoid
unnecessary pain
and lives not worthy of it
All of this loneliness
Waking nights of
stress and anguish
Impatience and frustration
from the anticipation of it
But then another question
comes just as it starts slipping
through your fingers
As you grasp around it
and feel as though
this is something
you possess for once
Begging you
to really know for sure

Before you are connected
Do you really want this?
What future is it
Could you stand his reality?
What exactly is that?
Where does he go
when you're left alone?
Falling for thoughts of obscurity
And random bouts of knowledge,
Impulsivity and creative discovery
Do you feel it already?
Creeping in slowly
Understanding and relief of existing
For the first time in your entire life
Someone actually wants to understand
Does he?
Only trusting the tests of time
Putting out no risk
of over vulnerability
Finding no one worthy of tears
No energy given
to those seeking to steal it
To use for some weird healing
No saviors found here
For the first time maybe
Is that truly what you feel and see here?
Pure intention
No alternative motivation
Only admiration

Have you figured it out yet?
Do you know what love is?
The journey for true discernment
hasn't been easy
Many mistakes have been made
In practice and living
What do you want from me?
Can two worlds
that are fully whole
truly be and seek
and find co-existence?
Am I that brave?
Do I find courage in this?
Is it better knowing you'll be hurt?
Or is it the opposite?
Not knowing at all finally
Going in complete terrified
Knowing how this could go
For the first time in my life
I'm finding faith in this
I actually believe that this
could be something worthy of me
The conversations with creation
 Could only give me
My small understanding
Begging me to go further than this
And we continue
So could you be a part of that?
Part of me believes that you could

That you've been further and seen more
I don't think that's crazy
I think you're just braver
Maybe you've done it
Not here to learn better
No atoning for my sins
Or used to discover myself
No lesson or test for perfection
I could never lie to you
I could only be known by you
I feel satisfied in this journey
No searching for better
 in another universe
Earth feels okay for once
Do you know who I am?
Does someone finally recognize me?
God, you're the only one who knows
And for the first time in all of history
I'm okay with it
Some things better left unspoken
We'll talk with our living
In our actions
The way you look at me and I stare back
The way you move in me
It's better letting things
work out on their own
with no outside intervention
So are we human?
Or are we dancers

I guess we'll find out
When we dance together
For the first time ever
Love will save the world
So let's save our world with it

Make Proud

I tried to make you proud
Striving for love
In the form of being
someone of significance
Forever reaching for status
Success in the form
Of something to brag about
Trying to do something
That you would finally admire
Maybe if I graduated college
If I got married and had a family
Joined your church and
rose up in leadership
Started a ministry and
 helped the homeless
Would you finally
give me what I crave?
Did I finally earn all your love, care, affection
and attention?
Would you finally want
to be close to me?
Giving me love
in the form of providing for me
Kicking and screaming
Performing and self hating
Never being good enough

Disgusted by my own humanity
What am I supposed
to do about that?
Give you the best performance
Keep a happy face
Make sure you
never see my true self
Forever hiding and
playing make believe
To keep you at ease
Help you sleep at night
Knowing your little girl
Became everything
you created her to be
Never truly known
Keep it professional
Unbiased as possible
Business as usual
Just another social structure
A construct, a system of control
Fall in line and be
The perfect daughter
More ladylike and proper
Don't let anyone see
How bad the storm inside
Destroys everything in sight
Ending all intimacy
Decimating friendships
That weren't very friendly

Just when you decide
To let them in
You lose everything
Call the chaos love
Praising your sacrifice
But I cried and
was killed internally
By the lack of being alive
Watching you
give up everything
That wakes you
from your sleep
These suicidal tendencies
Only break my heart
Break my mind
Why does your love
feel like hate to me?
Your control feels like despise
Overly inhumane rules
and restrictions on my existence
Seek sure destruction
To never be able to
Live and simply be
Drawing lines in the sand
Asking you to lie
If you want to
keep me in your life
Not interested in you
what's so ever

Wrong motivations
 interrupting closeness
Steering the conversation
Towards your perfect plan
So careful and controlling
All to ensure
You get what you want
So you can post online
To properly display
The life you're trying to convey
To brag and caption
 the moment
 #goals on Instagram
Inspiring constant dissatisfaction
Make everyone sick
Of their own existence
Sell them their dreams
Make them believe
It could be better
than what you have
Causing you to miss
 your present moment
Taking you outside of everything
Convince them to work harder
Turn their dreams of contentment
Into dreams of labor
Make the rat race look attractive
You could have all
of your hearts desires

If you give up
everything you are
To be everything you're not
Finally then
You'll achieve
the American dystopian reality
of comfort and safety
None living dreams
Of isolation and solidarity
Better this way
True empathy is a threat
To automated hive mentality
Let them sleep
Welcome to retirement
Stop your striving
No more chasing the wind
Sleep more, eat, and pray
You'll survive and be okay
Find peace in accepting
and loving the role
 you've been given